To those who have ever felt silenced, may your voice be heard

Love, Me

Gideon Faku

Published by Gideon Faku, 2024.

LOVE, ME

First edition. November 18, 2024.

ISBN: 979-8230143659

Written by Gideon Faku.

Table of Contents

To my dog Sam, my faithful companion and dear friend, who left paw prints on my heart. May your memory forever be cherished

"The deepest pain is the pain of bieng unseen."- John O'Donohue

I am a new young writer & I started writing this book when I was 15, as a means to help people from my past trauma experiences, which is how this book was born.

If am not writing in my desk at home, I am constantly having adventures on my own, working on my Film production company, reading, playing video games, going for walks or playing basketball at the park, spending time with my dogs, and most importantly spending time with my family.

Keep in touch via the web:

Instagram: https://www.instagram.com/parivus_films01/

YouTube: https://www.youtube.com/@parivusfilms

Email: boeterjames@gmail.com

Or call: 078 017 0881

Over all, I hope you enjoy reading the book & I look forward to hearing what your thoughts are after reading it!

To my parents, thank you for all you've ever done for me,
The teachings and support means the most

To my siblings, thank you for all the joy of laughter and love you've poured unto me

LOVE,
ME

Keep your softness, stay gentle and remain kind. Don't let the ugly around you make you bitter

After reading this little book I hope you go all in on yourself. I hope you listen to that quiet voice within, to the soft nudges, to the inner child in you that just knows. I hope you trust it knowing what feels right even when it scares you, and when the voice of fear asks "But what if it doesn't work out?" I hope you listen to the voice that responds, "But what if it does?" I Hope you let go of the fear and all the negative thoughts that you have, I hope whisper of courage rises from the ashes of everything that could've broken you but didn't, that it reminds you of how strong you are and that your spirit irrepressible. That you are brave and capable. That actually, everything you need to follow your heart-led path already exists within you, and I hope that you say yes to your dreams and treat them like they're the most real, most fragile, truest things to exist, I hope you claim them. That you know that deep within they are already yours. And I hope that you know that you are in control of your mind and thoughts, and stay true to yourself who you are above everything else. I hope that you choose yourself every single day, I hope that you take care of your heart and most lastly I hope that you change the world with your smile but never let the world change your smile

With love,

Gideon

Introduction

THE STRUGGLE IS REAL

I used to be bullied by other kids & sometimes by even adults, strangers, people would make fun of how I looked whether that was my skin complexion or the colour of my eyes & all these negative energies that I was exposed to made me a quieter person with a low self-esteem, confidence in myself, and I started having anxiety when I would be around people because of the trauma I mean don't get me wrong my family life was amazing, I have two loving wonderful parents who always did their best to make sure I had a normal childhood which is filled with joy and love, I have two amazing siblings a younger sister and my older brother, life at home is great, but the chaos that changed me came from the outside world, from people. People that try to put you down, growing up around these people made it almost much difficult to breathe, I felt like the negative chapter of my life would never end because the negativity they poured had an impact that made me become a closed person that had a hard time letting go of the negativity that I was consuming.

I became tired of living my life in fear of people and negativity, I knew if I continued listening to these thoughts instead of facing them I would become a person I wouldn't recognize, so I told myself that it was time to change my life & face the trauma and all the negative noise that was in my head.

This journey definitely was hard, I felt like I wouldn't be able to overcome the noise

and have a much healthier positive mind but I kept going, and with much support from my family and friends I walked through it & while in that Journey I had a revelation which made me think to myself If I could overcome this, then maybe other people can too so that's how the book idea was born, I know that there's a lot of people struggling out there in the world, and are seeking help but no one is listening but my purpose for this book is to help you guys with my experience & I hope this book becomes the support for you.

PART 1

UNDERSTANDING NEGATIVE THOUGHTS

The voice in Your Head

Negative thoughts about ourselves come in our lives in many different ways, whether it's from our upbringing, the places we go to, the people we around, our influences, including our parents, and the more we have these negative thoughts our brain starts accumulating that and it keeps it which leads us to believing whatever negative thing we tell to ourselves, funny how the brain works right? We get into these bad habits and thoughts like a comfortable bed, easy to get into but hard to get out of. When we look at ourselves in the mirror instead of telling yourself how great you are and God created wonderful human being.

We don't usually like what we see, we've let the outside noise consume us which led us to believe we the bar was set to high and we will never get to where we want to be in life which is the best versions of ourselves and not caring about what people say if we would be honest with ourselves we can achieve almost anything we set our mind to, and its true because you reading this right now because you've set your mind to believe what the world told you right? Nothing kills you faster than your own mind so you have to learn to not stress over things that are out of your control.

Now you probably wondering how do I know this, I know this because I've gone through it, trying to find success in a new dark age led to many trials and tribulations because of the places I would go to, the closest of people often telling me I'm not enough, I am ugly, I will never make anyone proud, my body is ugly, all those words led me to being insecure, which somehow I started to believe them and my brain connected with that and that's where I developed my (OCD) is a long-lasting disorder in which a person experiences uncontrollable and recurring thoughts (obsessions), engages in repetitive behaviours (compulsions), or both and as a person with OCD you can only imagine how painful that was, 24/7 my head would have all these voices that I am really never going to succeed and that I deserve to die, and the war with the brain is the most hardest battle ever, I have lost against my mind so many times and even now I am still on the journey to controlling these thoughts and that the outside noise can dome no harm and that I am enough, because I am and you are too, Battling your own thoughts and finding success is going to be a hard journey but it is achievable but it requires dedication and discipline as we go through this journey you going to see yourself all over the place, you going to have to trust in the hall of hearts, and believe that you can achieve this battle with yourself and be happier than before, my promise to you is that I will try my best to help you become a better, disciplined, happier version of yourself because I know how hard and painful it is to go through the negative thoughts and having the closest of people making you feel less confident in yourself but the ultimate truth is we all have the ability to come from nothing to something, step by step, day by day, the results will come, and if anyone is magically going to appear and just suddenly make your life better, just know that person is always going to be you, this will be a long journey but I hope you'll listen, and if you start overthinking again and having those thoughts that you won't be able to achieve this goal just as much as I had them while writing this book tell yourself "you overthinking again. Breathe. It's okay, you'll figure it out and if you don't that's okay too

Defining where the negativity starts

We've all had the golden age where it was the best years of our lives, I mean we all come from different aspects of life and beginnings, our childhood for most are the years we loved and cared more about the small things rather than the difficult things. Two different things. The only most stressful thing I'd get worried about as a kid was coming from playing with friends riding our bikes as the sunset on our ways head back home late, it's funny I know but that's the only thing I was ever worried about. And as I grew older over what seems to be years ago it makes me just think...where did the Golden days go? You might have heard this expression time and time again because it's true.

The truth is we all miss our childhood no matter how rough or painful it was, we miss those bike rides with our friends. Waking up in the morning full of energy as the sun hits our window and we smell food through the hall leading to the kitchen and mom is cooking.

"This is going to be a good day", when our friends would come fetch us for a ride down the neighbourhood and we meet more kids and they tag along and we all find ourselves playing together. Familiar right?

I know it, you know what I'm talking about. As I write this chapter it makes me chuckle a little as I look back to those days and I hope it does the same for you too. Now I asked the question, where did those Golden days go? The truth is they didn't go anywhere, shocking right? But you see the truth is there still here all around us, through pictures, through music, nature, skies, flowers, butterflies, People etc.

The difficulties of today's age have changed that for us and we accepted that and we moved forward. The beauty of life is still in the small things, it's still in family, "Ubuntu" a philosophy that means the act of acting together, helping each other, and it could mean having a strong foundation for family, the good thing is it could mean anything to everyone.

We often let the difficulties takeover and control how we live and we don't focus on the positive things that could lead to more positivity. It's easy to get caught up in the past or worry about the future. But in fact, no amount of regret can change what's already happened, and no level of anxiety can control what's to come. The beauty of life lies in the imperfect present.

Remember the quote "**even the darkest nights eventually give way to the rising sun**". Our childhood holds a special place in our hearts because we made it great, now closely pay attention I said "we" the truth is it wasn't all sunshine and rainbows, we've had our fair share of trouble but we didn't let that define us, we faced those difficulties head on, we all lose people growing up, we cry, we celebrate, we laugh and life goes on

LOVE,
ME

So our lives today is driven by difficulties and challenges and we've let them take over. I'm guilty of that, we all should be. Life is too short to be worried about the things we can't control. That's why we miss our childhood so much, it's because we paused and looked around, we never let the bad things control everything we lived simply and we with each other and set differences aside. The childhood friends we had down the street, we were all different but we didn't care about being different, we cared about playing outside with the ball, buying all the water toy guns, and jumping in the pool or exploring the neighbourhood with family relatives, these things are still there with us but we live in a time where those difficulties control us instead of us controlling them, kids nowadays don't even go outside or at least in my hometown, it's like everyone is glued to their phones and the longer they do that the longer the difficulties grow and the longer depression kicks in because of what we face in technology, and our mind starts accumulating that and it turmoil our souls, and the more we glued to these technologies the faster time passes than we even realize. It's a dark new age and we have let it take over, that's why we have so much negativity in our lives, I remember this one time I had felt so lonely which is something we all feel, and my friend introduced me to sites where you can talk with different people from around the world, and I was so invested and interested in that because I thought talking with people online would change that, you see I was a shy quiet person growing up and that developed over time and I was in this closet of being afraid of talking to people, we'll get on this as we go on. So as the quiet person who felt lonely I got excited and I started talking to different people online and what happened was two things, I realized the world is full of negativity, it doesn't matter what part, except for the Philippines of course, they still live as simply as they can and I admire that. The second thing I realized was that the lonely feeling would never go away just because of that. I mean don't get me wrong, it was fun talking to people whenever that feeling of loneliness hit and I met a few people that were genuinely kind but that feeling never got away. It never does, we all feel lonely but the most important thing I learned was the best way to overcome these battles is within ourselves, the loneliness I felt started disappearing when I spent more time learning about myself, putting the phone down and going for a walk or even playing with my dogs made me feel maybe there's still a light in this dark age. I learnt that mama was right when she told us to put our phones down and be in the moment because she knew it would grow with us, the addiction, the technology, and the most important one 'Time' would pass by like a butterfly, It flies never to be regained, it's a luxury the one we spend filled with negativity and darkness instead of quality time with our family and friends. As kids we weren't glued to technology, we may have played video games but now I think I understand why our parents always had a bedtime for us, so we could get good sleep and get ready for the next day and adventure that awaits us.

I now know why they told us to switch off the TV after 8pm, now I know why they told us to go places with them and strive to be outside your comfort zone. I wish I had listened, but because of how we spend our time is in our control, I still have the chance and so can you.

Everything affects us, even our childhood and upbringing. No matter how golden it was, no one is perfect or has lived a perfect life because I for one am yet to meet a human who's had perfect existence, I don't think that person exists, growing up had its own battles and negativity, as a black light skin kid growing up in coloured areas, it was tough, people looked at your character or personality based off your skin colour, and that created a negative space in my head that I never realized until I started learning more about myself. Back in my earlier years, of school, as a child I was so excited to meet other kids and create friendships not knowing that feeling of excitement would change to become fear but it became the opposite.

I was quiet shy kid & in school people often saw the quiet kid "weird", I have no idea why, but because of that and also being shy which I am now guilty of, it lead to people picking on me and making fun of me or how I looked and my skin colour, eye colour, all of the things that didn't make sense for someone to be make fun off, and every day coming back home my parents would ask me how my day at school went and sometimes I would suck it all up and tell them it was good and I would hide the pain, but I think they noticed that I would sometimes cry in my room and what I didn't realize was the pain I kept hidden demanded to be uncaged and felt. Somehow the unique kids would always be made fun of or bullied and my dad used to tell me that **"people treated me in an unkind way because people's brains are rewired in a way that when they see someone or something unique they label it and try to torture it because they don't understand**

it" and for the longest time growing up I thought he said this as a way of making me feel better but now I know he was right, I wish I knew that sooner, but I took that pain and I did what any human shouldn't and I hid it, but I wouldn't blame myself for doing that because I was a kid, I didn't know about holding resentment towards the people who hurt us, I didn't know that crying was okay, and that sometimes letting your guard down you open yourself to love.

It's amazing that something that happens in a second can change your whole lifetime, holding resentment towards those people made me have a hard time to forgive, but I had to because in order to move forward and let negativity go we have to forgive the ones that hurt us in order for healing to endure.it made me mad for a long time though how the world is shaped to hurt people hurt people instead of love people love people, that broke me to the core but it taught me so much about how the outside noise and what we hear can affect us and shape us even if we don't notice for the longest time I locked myself away from people and would sometimes be ion my room all day and developed these habits because of the negative thoughts that controlled how I started living, I would try to find ways to change myself or how I look so I wouldn't be made fun of, I would sometimes put makeup on to make myself more tractive, and did this everyday but I didn't like it, I had let the outside noise dictate how I would live my life, negative thoughts, fear and insecurity.

What I felt in the inside was far more different than the outside, I had consumed this negative energy from negative people and that can turmoil our souls, and as children of God we must remember that everywhere we go we consume a piece of it with our spirits. Sometimes I think about how different my life could've been had I not went through all the negative noise. Maybe being told that I am God's beautiful creation and that I am enough I would have never had to battle these thoughts and I would be self-loving., I longed to be told I am enough and that I am loved until I had to learn to tell myself that, **so in order to live a happier life coming from a situation like this our happiness and confidence should not rely on others, you should tell yourself you beautiful and how wonderfully created you are** instead of bringing each other down we should motivate each other

It's easy to get caught up in the past or worry about the future, but in fact, no amount of regret can change what's already happened, but we can change who we are or where we going, just like the legend Doc from the classic movies Back to the future said, "your future is whatever you make it, so make it a good one."

No level of anxiety can control what's to come. The beauty of life is the imperfect present. Remember, even the darkest nights eventually give way to the sunrise.

So, instead of letting the weight of yesterday or the uncertainty of tomorrow taunt you, appreciate the messy, unpredictable beauty of now. Life unfolds in the present, and sometimes, all you need is to take step back, breathe, and trust that, just like the night making room for the dawn, our current challenges will make way for brighter moments. Embrace the imperfections, navigate through the uncertainties, and let the unfolding chapters of your life be a testament to your resilience and Adaptability.

What holds us back from breaking these thoughts and addictive cycle? It's within, now what do I mean by this? its within ourselves, the person holding you back is you, although the negative thoughts came outside from people and what we consume, the person who can change this is in the inside and that's you and if you don't take action sooner you will suffer the pain of regret by living your life in a sense of fear and letting those words of negativity control how you live your life.

As we go on in this journey of life I started learning to realize that no one cares what you do with your life, yes our parents and the ones who care about us try to put us in the right direction when we find ourselves lacking but what I am saying is whether you keep going or quit no one is going to care but you.

We face all these challenges in life and life goes on, I spent over years insecure about the way that I look and with fear because of the negative thoughts that was created when I let the world control how I move and see myself and I would go to bed and when my head would hit the pillow at night all the thoughts came in, fear.. fear, and as a person with OCD it would make me not feel secure even in my own home and I would not feel safe everywhere I went because I would compare myself with people and have dark thoughts and all those what if's and to break from this you have "if asked you to name all the things that you love, how long would it take for you to name yourself? You probably wouldn't even think about yourself, heck when I started this journey I wouldn't even be on the list back then I would probably name 10 things including people before I'd even think of myself but here's the thing I do love myself as much as anyone can love themselves, because the reality is that it brings me joy to write-down others names and appreciate what they have done for me and you never know there's someone out there who would write your name too because they see your value even if you couldn't and they know you beautiful and loved, it may be your parent, your closest friends, or even your neighbour, but because of what we have consumed in our minds that we aren't enough we believed it so you probably saying to yourself it's crazy for me to assume you would, that's how our minds work they listen, they take in and they never turn off,

Steve Harvey once said "you have to change the way you think it is the whole determining factor of where you go in life"

The things we listen to eventually become born into reality.

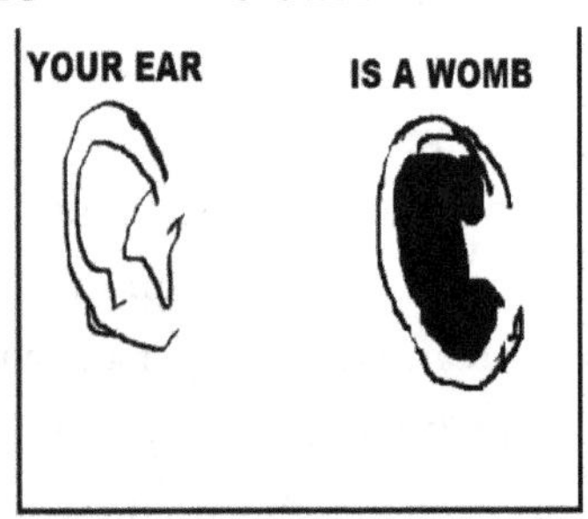

THE COMPARISON TRAP

"It's not what you look at that matters, it's what you see." ~ Henry David Thoreau

A Change in perspective leads to positive changes

As I go on through my journey battling negativity with myself I've learnt that your perspective to how you live your life and see the world is everything. Thinking about understanding something , your life can be based on negativity because of what was said and what your mind created but the perspective with that is created by you, how are you going to see it, what attitude point of view are you going to have towards all these challenges life gives us as a go on my journey of the negative thought which led to insecurity about myself was because I had let people who felt a certain way about themselves control how I looked at myself, growing up around people who bullied me either it was in school or kids I would meet whatever they said that hurt me because to me it was always confusing how at home I would be treated normally as I am and loved, but then when I'm out in the world you would hear people say things to bring you down and I think part of the reason why people bully others is because of jealousy towards them and it's because that person is unique so when something is unique and they don't understand it, they will try to torture it, and I started believing these words and I thought maybe what they are saying is true, and my perspective in life changed immensely, I saw myself the way that they did or tried to make me see myself which is ugly, weird and thinking of it always brings me down, and I tried so many ways to fit in with them but they still didn't stop and I couldn't understand why, if you don't form a strong opinion about yourself you brain will start internalizing what others think of you, you'll begin to believe that you are so much less than you actually because you are what you believe yourself to be, this is the power of the mind, to recreate that vision you must create a vision of yourself so clear that it can't be blurred by the fog of people's opinions If you get to choose something, ensure you put your heart and brain to it. We oftentimes try to fit into social circles, peer activities just because that is something that makes you more 'likeable'. Feel free to exit such scenarios and free up your mental space. If there are people who don't match your vibe even after trying your best, leave them. People who bring you down, gaslight the situation, aren't worth your time and energy. Under lot of situations, it might happen that two people are looking at a problem from different angles, for example the famous 6 and 9. It's literally just a matter of perspective. It's important to understand when to argue and when to discuss. Not every battle needs to be fought so in a situation where you find yourself battling negative thoughts on whether you can achieve something or success, whatever you want to call it. Tell yourself you can do it, tell yourself whatever negative words was said about you to break you, tell yourself it will make you stronger, When you feeling the highest of lows and can't move forward, you can.

Change your perspective and move forward, if you lost someone you thought you'd spend the rest of your life with your spouse then they betray you and you depressed because of that, remember that when one door closes another one opens, you see how that changes your point of view? Have you ever found yourself with a group of friends that you didn't feel comfortable around or the same scenarios of bad energy would happen over and over again and you called them out on it and they stopped hanging out with your or being your friend, and you depressed about it, think yourself out of it. Think that maybe God removed those people in my life because they weren't right for me, and that sometimes we lose certain people to find ourselves and then we will find our people, the ones that will love us the way we want to be loved, cherish us and appreciate us, it's all in Perspective. How you think of situations and the difficulties we face in life, the negative thoughts we have about ourselves, the fears that people put upon us and if you change your perspective you can then start to realize that you in control of how you see things, because you are.

Quote of the day:

"The mind is always against you when you want to change something in your life, it always shows out when you want to show up

THE JOURNEY OF JOURNALING

"Start writing, no matter what. The water does not flow until the faucet is turned on"

J

journaling is one of the best way to fight the thoughts or pain you hold inside, as I went through my journey of the negative thoughts I had and OCD frustrations, I started writing these thoughts down, it doesn't matter how you write them, whether in poetry, or in a song, when you write down what you feeling it's the same as speaking about them except you journaling, it helped me so much through my negative thoughts that led to my frustrations and I sometimes got so angry and wished I could turn the brain off, but I looked for alternatives to do that and as much as I know therapy helps and speaking to someone it makes me feel like a burden, and I know it shouldn't so I found my own therapy which helped because every time I would write, my heart would let out all the pain and I would often cry, but here's the thing, if you cry it shows progress, and it means you letting all the pain out instead of holding everything in.

I wrote every day for what seemed to be a year and it felt like journaling cleansed me, the thoughts were more bearable, so journal, write all that you think or feel. Embrace the emotions and be zen, you are what you believe yourself to be, if you think you ugly write down that thought and write I'm beautiful, feel all that you feeling and cry as much as you can. That's how self-love is developed, self-love is by teaching yourself, body and most importantly your mind that you are all these amazing things and then they become reality, this became a life changer as I kept journaling & little did I know that I would be healing. All the broken parts that were once pieces, became a puzzle I learnt how to solve

Journaling can help with healing negative thoughts by:

Creating Distance

`It can create open space from your thoughts and feelings. Which would then allow you to reflect easily, and by identifying these negative thought patterns and triggers, which you can then learn to challenge them and change.

Identifying negative thoughts

Journaling can help you identify negative thoughts and behaviours. And give an opportunity for a different outlook

Organizing thoughts

Writing naturally is a form of healing as it forces you to organize your thoughts into a sequence, which can help you understand the cause and effect of these thoughts

Processing experiences

Writing about challenging experiences can help you process them in a constructive way, and make it easier to handle difficult emotions.

Tracking symptoms

Keeping a daily log of your symptoms can help you identify & recognize, triggers and teach you how to control them

So Journaling is very important in our everyday lives as it can gives us new perspectives, it can naturally identify all these thoughts, triggers & where they are coming from while healing those bits and shaping them in a box that you can intuitively open, close and control

“If you lucky enough to feel sad, savour it while it lasts. If only it means you cared about something hard enough you let it under your skin~ John Keoing

Quote for the day

Don't take criticism from people you wouldn't go to for advice

Dear younger Me,

I haven't let you go yet I've been longing to write to you, but I couldn't quite find the right words because I was scared.

I first would like to tell you how much life has changed ever since you grew up, things are much harder than before, which makes me miss the days you'd play with no care in the world, but because of how time has passed it helps me apreciatte the moments even more. I want you to know that im sorry for all the pain you had to endure. im sorry for all the negative things people would say to you, I still remember how you cried that night, that it broke you, im sorry that people couldn't quite understand you because of how unique God created you, and how you had to hold so much resentment without even knowing when all you wanted was to fit in, but you never did, even now you still don't, but that's okay. I've now learnt from all the pain and that sometimes forgiving people that hurt us and letting go of the negativity helps us move forward, your connection with yourself grew and you much confident now, or atleast you working on it. parents are much more supportive and you love your sister and brother even more now & building a better relationship with them, you journal alot now and you still following your dreams, I wish I had protected you through those times of suffering, I wish I was more confident and not let the outside noise break you on the inside, I still keep a part of you everywhere I go Thank you for all the times that we shared, I will miss the light that you brought into my life always I love you for all that makes you, you

With ever lasting love,

Your future self

This was part of my journaling which we'll share more of as we go on, I had this idea of writing to a younger version of me. the things I would say, do with if I ever met my past younger self, and honestly this letter said it all, while writing it helped me remember where I came from, notice how different I am than I was yesterday, it I learnt about the pain I was carrying as a kid, how it shaped me into the person I am today and how the experiences I went through made me stronger, which then if I could go back in time I would protect my young self with every power and strength that I have now so that person would not have to go through the same pain.

Daily Journal

Reflect:

After writing in the Journal page I want you to reflect by ticking in these boxes

While writing the letter I noticed how different I am from when I was a child

While writing I noticed I am still the same person who managed to control the pain as years went by

The pain and negativity I experienced made me who I am today in a good impactful way

While writing I noticed where all the negative patterns came from

The pain and negativity I experienced made me who I am today in a bad way

I have a better relationship with my parents now as opposed to then

Do I wish I had protected the younger version of myself?

The negative experiences I had growing up do not have an impact in how my mind functions now

Would I have preferred not experiencing negativity and not gone through the

I have never cared of what people say & I

experience today?	don't let the negative thoughts control me than I did then

If you ticked few of the boxes you in the right place learning wise and you have grown but if you have ticked less, you need to start changing your ways because if you still in the same spot as you were then IT'S A SERIOUS PROBLEM. But don't worry though I will help you navigate this and start learning ways to move forward.

WISDOM TO START THE DAY:

Appreciate everyday of your life, Good days give memories and Bad days give lessons but they offer lessons that shape your character and teach you how to be strong, patient & better,

Fear, anxiety, and Doubt

Illustration by Fiona Montanez

The way we grow up has a toll on us far more than we can imagine, It's like a woman living with an abusive husband, As she keeps experiencing the violence she starts being insecure about her body which makes her wonder why her husband says all these negative things to her, why he acts violent towards her and she starts overthinking, as she does this her mind starts accumulating these thoughts which leads her to believe she is all the things her husband says to her, the scars in her body makes her think maybe I'm really not beautiful and I deserve all this pain which obviously is not true but that's how experiences have an impact on the way we think

As the abusive we want to make our victims fear to say "No, enough is enough" and for some reason we as the victims are to blame and let me elaborate on why I say this The fear instilled in us is in our control whether we let it define us and not speak up, hold resentment towards the ones that hurt us which creates a turmoil on its own, whether we let it determine how we will live our lives just like superheroes live their lives, they live it according to helping people so they won't have to go through the same pain as they did because they know how much that sucked, Whereas for villains they let the pain control them and they hold the resentment which makes them want to revenge or fight back, or even kill the people who have hurt us.

So we should be guilty of how we let the pain control us. The Abuser acts the way they do towards us so they can feel in control which is why the victim feels fear and all the thoughts control them. As humans we have to be able to say "No, enough is enough" We have to have the courage to speak up, the courage to walk away, We are created in a supernatural way that we can control ourselves, whatever you go through you always pull through right? Because that's how we were created to be strong enough to be in control of ourselves, the longer you keep all the pain stored inside it will change you to the point where you someone you don't notice, a person you weren't before. I understand that all these traumatic experiences are absolutely fucking hard and if it was up to me I wouldn't even let you go through them especially as a kid who just wants to experience childhood in a positive outlook, but sometimes we go through these experiences so we can be strong emotionally to tackle problems,

We need not let these experiences define us nor should they make us, instead look at them as teachings and maybe your path in life is top help other people who have gone through the same experiences as you too, but you can't help anyone until you learn to help yourself. I believe I went through all the pain I did as a child so I could then change other people's lives, and find my purpose, which is why I wrote this book So I could change a life of someone going through the same challenges, the ones who want to learn to control their pain, and change their lives so they could do the same for others, Be the point of difference because You are your own superhero and I believe you can be a hero for others too.

PART 2

BREAKING FREE

'Stand grounded in your truth, let your light expand, and watch your spirit soar with limitless potential.' -William

Reframing negative thoughts

Holding Resentment is like holding a knife with both your hands firmly as you bleeding, you hate the pain but you never let go, that's not a good position to be in is it? It's not because the more you hold on to that knife, you cut and you bleed and eventually you'll lose blood. Holding resentment is like that for me. Growing up and experiencing all the negativity around me whether it was someone making fun of how I look, my skin colour, eye colour, What I never realized was I was holding all that pain and had resentment towards them, which at first seemed okay because if someone or something hurts you, you feel a certain way around that, you more cautious even about the way you act, so to me it was normal at first but as time went on that resentment grew and I noticed I would have outbursts around those certain people and I didn't notice where that came from or how it came about at this point of time I wasn't as aware emotionally towards these feelings I thought that they would pass, but little did I know they would grow, day after day, I became bitter and bitter it wasn't after until I listened to one of my favourite podcasts, They were talking about how the resentment we have towards the ones who hurt us can control us I realized why I had so much anger in me screaming to be let out, every time I would be around these people I would be in safety mode and I had to learn to forgive them, it's easier said than done I know, but it's part of the journey so it must happen. How do you let go of the resentment? You start by saying I forgive you. Now I'm not saying you have to go back to these people and speak to them face to face, but find alternatives which I will give below, find alternatives that help you forgive them and telling those people that:

"I forgive you for all the pain that you caused me, although it changed me in whatever way, I had enough time to process this through and I've realized that holding all the cautiousness and being resentful towards you only made things harder for me so in order for me to heal I choose to let go of all the things you did to me which I won't exclusively mention I understand you were also going through problems with yourself which is why I forgive you, but with that said, I don't want any connections or anything to do with you I've had enough and you have no choice but to respect this decision because whether you like it or not you have no control over this situation now"

That wasn't so hard was it? You see how powerful it feels to stand ground and be in control? For a second there I felt like I am superman because I am, we are humans who need to take control and remove what doesn't help us grow and let room for improvement.

Now saying these words and speaking them into existence can help you start finding ways to move forward and embrace the new, all the heavy luggage of resentment only holds you back until you actively take action.

Ask yourself what happens when I decide I am qualified of good things, to be in control of who I let in my life and who doesn't get any form of access towards my life, what happens when I decide I am deserving of standing in my power and having the ability to walk away with no walls held up against these people, then you will start noticing changes. I had to learn the hard way in the act of forgiveness towards those people and I think I'm still learning to forgive. Sometimes I tell myself I forgave these people, but other times I tell myself I haven't, And if you also experience these feelings, that's okay. The way I had to learn that I should let these walls I created up was through relationships which shouldn't have been because I was hurting many people I love by having these walls up.

Sometimes I wouldn't go out of my room the whole day, sometimes I would have so much anger thinking of those times which would lead me acting excessively towards my parents or siblings, I would have all these mood swings which I am guilty of because I was hurting the ones who were trying to help me and this became a pattern, I would have all the feelings and feel like punching something or breaking a glass and it would release frustration but it wasn't helpful in any way.

My parents were worried about me and that's when I realized I can't keep holding up these walls towards a part of the world that just wanted to love me and love and love me for being who I was, Kind, generous and loving.

Have I lost relationships because of these actions? Absolutely. Am I guilty of this? Definitely, Do I wish I would have let these walls down and let the resentment go so I would've been more present, loving and nurturing towards these relationships and friendships? With every bit of my soul a thousand percent.

So embrace the pain, let go of resentment, break down the walls and while doing that make sure you take care of all these relationships because they are also fragile. Here are alternatives that worked for me

1. Write a letter towards your abuser and say everything and not leave anything out and send it to them, after that what will happen is you will feel a shift change or feel like you've just removed carrying so much luggage on your back. If you don't want to go this route that's totally fine.

1. Write a letter towards your abuser and express yourself and all the pain and bury it somewhere you'll never go back again. This one is definitely weird but it totally works

1. Write down all your feelings to yourself for example "I forgive you for all the pain so I can learn to move forward" keep writing this and read it every-day and speak it into existence

Get yourself a punching bag and become active, whenever you feel frustrated, punch the bag as many times as you want to until you feel tired. This one has worked so much for me because it helps you release the frustrations and pain

Screaming all the negative words out sometimes helps we release all these toxic feelings we have, but this one should be done in a place far from people so you can feel all the feels and cry if you need to.

Prayer worked for me. Speaking to God and asking him to help you let go of these feelings towards people and prayer naturally makes us feel better no matter how many minutes we spend praying we feel much better after as praying is known to cleanse our souls from all the darkness in the world. So pray, speak to God and he will listen.

“Sometimes as humans, we have a tendency to bleed on the ones who didn’t break us”

"So many
Things we do stems from
How we grew up"

Growing up I was a very sensitive kid, partially because of my insecurity of being different from other kids & all the noise that came with that destroyed my self-esteem & I hate thinking about those moments of being bullied, made fun of you name it. I never quite understood why kids would make fun of others kids, I still don't quite get it to this day. It doesn't make sense, why would another human being make fun of how someone was created when we all were created in the same way but with our own special different features? Because I sometimes wonder if I looked just like them would they have not made fun of me? Probably not. But why did they? Because they saw the sensitive quiet kid and thought they had no strength or could stand up for themselves and truthfully speaking they were right I couldn't because they had instilled fear in me that made me lose confidence in myself and feel unsafe in most environments.

The only time I ever felt a bit of peace of mind was when I got home from School because at home they always treated me the same as my siblings because that's how it should be, We were all special with all our differences and something that I am forever so grateful for is that my siblings always told me "you should never try to fit in when you were born to stand out" growing up at home wasn't as hard as the world outside, I mean they were conflicts here and there as any other family

but after all that we were always supportive of each other and I think every-time I came home with tears on my face, my siblings always tried their best to carry that pain with me and I am forever grateful for that.

Do I hate thinking of those moments? Totally but a part of make now is grateful that I had gone through them because I learnt many lessons from them, It made me stronger, I connected with myself spiritually and most importantly I started praying more to God.

Now I am not saying that the way people treated me negatively was okay, I wouldn't wish that for anyone, If you have the voice and courage to walk away from an experience like that, I suggest you do it But if you have undergone these experiences as a kid or whether you going through the same experiences right now I hope this book becomes a blueprint to help you see it through and not give up.

These experiences teach us so much about why people treat us the way that they do or why we are the ones that go through it. It's because God has a plan for us, but It's is up to you how you'll pursue it.

Letting go of these habits is going to be a long stretch and you have to work hard, if you not willing to put in the work, then this book is not for you, but if you are ready to overcome the noise and change your way of thinking I'm glad you here, like I said letting go of these habits is hard, It's an addiction equal to a drug, when you try to let go, you suffer, for example a person with an alcohol addiction suffers when try withdraw from drinking and the withdrawal symptoms include, tremors, sweating, hallucinations & feel the need to drink

But with dedication and help it is possible to be healthy and in control of yourself again, the same applies to these negative thoughts we have. For OCD people it can be quite difficult too, once it starts it's hard to stop, you have all these thoughts in your head of what ifs and when you try to stop overthinking your mind is filled with too many negative thoughts at once, you can imagine how frustrating that can be, my first try was the most difficult one.

I was at home and I started asking myself what if I could just close my eyes, breathe in and let the thoughts go away, and for quite a while mindfulness worked but then they came flashing like a train in a blink of an eye they were back again, that's how addictions work sometimes we try to believe they are gone but without proper treatment they come back even more stronger, we need to hear these thoughts, identify where they come from and not ignore them as they will be stored in the back of your mind.

Think of a box filled with memories as time goes on the memories grow, but we must remember when we let go of something, another one comes in and that's a good thing, we should not feel scared to let go of these addictions even if we adapted and this is the way we living, that's the worst way to live. Bad habits can kill you and I mean this literally, although it may not mean on the outside but definitely on the inside. **"If you want to move to a higher level of life, you have to be willing to let go of some of your old ways of thinking and being and adopt new ones"- T. Harv Eker**

When you understand that every opinion is a vision loaded with personal history, you will begin to understand that all judgement is a confession

There's a reason why it feels so scary letting go of our past ways of living but it's necessary, I had too many bad habits before I had let go of them, some are probably still there as I'm figuring it out, I remember how much I hated going to the store with my parents as it would mean being around different people I didn't know, I'm in my room probably playing a game with my online friends or reading a book, I've always loved books as it was a way of escaping "Can you accompany me we going to the stores" my mom says, hearing these word was similar to a horrifying jump scare that makes your body feel absolute fear, literally, It felt like my body left my soul and as I hear them again the Negative thoughts transcend and my body goes into safe mode, I felt fear and as much as I didn't want to go, I had no choice so I put up my hoodie to hide my face and I go along with them, This turned into a habit, every time we would go to the stores or leave the house for even a mere second, I was in fear. I hated school events, School plays, Holiday events, Family gatherings, Funerals, Parties, Family days out, going to the stores, Parks, Interactions with strangers I hated all of them, not because I never once loved them, but because of the pain experienced in these places that made me doubt my ability.

How do we overcome the fear of putting ourselves out there?

You overcome it by putting yourself out there, and that's something I had to learn the hard way. My fear wasn't because of the world it was because of the people around it, the negativity I had consumed so I realized the only way to get away from this bubble is by not being afraid and expressing my self by using the power I hold.

As humans have power, the power of freedom, the power of free speech, the power of opinions, and the power of inspiring & the power of standing ground. I realized that just because people wouldn't stop being negative doesn't mean that everyone is the same as that, I learnt that there are people out there who would love me for who I am, and people who also want to inspire and motivate, but most of them are hard to find as they are also in the bubble the world has created for them, but they're out there and I hope you find them.

One of my best friends once said something that almost broke me down, not that what they said was painful but it was beautiful and wholesome, and it's been a long time since someone said something so genuine and impactful in a good way, we were having a conversation and she's the kind of person who loves having me around and introducing me to new people, she knows the loneliness I've felt in my life and she always makes sure I never feel left out, so here we are and I ask her "why do you love introducing me to new people?" I said, "Because you a treasure worth sharing" she said.

When I heard those words it felt like a huge wall I had held up had fallen down with the reassurance of "I belong" and that I have found people who accept me for who I am, not that I had tears rolling down my face but it made me feel wholesome and she will never know how much that changed my perspective, not just on negativity but on myself, It made me feel confident than I ever had been. It's difficult when you're listening to your fears. You are aware that the thoughts running through your head are killing you but you just need someone to listen to you and support you. You need someone to listen to you and support you. You need someone to calm the storm inside your head, someone who will take your hand and hold it against their chest. I hope you find a person who is willing to battle these demons with you, who will never see you as weird, but beautiful; as you are.

I hope you find a friend who will be understanding and reassuring, Someone to sit down with you, hold you & ask you why you believe that you not wonderfully created and promise you that they would never hurt you like the world has, and no matter how silly, or obvious things may seem, you never know what your reassurance can do for someone else.

Having these healthy relationships can also help us become healthier individuals because being around uplifting people make us feel better with ourselves. But we have to pick these relationships and friendships wisely & these true connections deepen with time, I learnt to let my guard down a little more and be myself within these people that I call my village. & coming from a place of anger, frustrations that led me to hurt these people that love me for me, these lessons helped do the best that I can, to give them the best that I am & it takes time and obsession.

Remember a ship is always safe at shore, but that's not what it is made for.

LOVE,
ME

Running and Exercise

Running and exercise worked wonders for me, and I felt that all this was not only about keeping the body healthy; it was a mental emancipation-a kind of therapy that really fixed my feet to the ground. What started off as a way of keeping fit soon turned out to be an investment that would help change the mind just as much as the body did? It became my quiet time, a place where my mind could drift and I could focus on nothing but the rhythm of my breathing and the sound of my feet touching the ground. Every step was like peeling layers and layers of stress, self-doubt, and negativity off me and leaving them all out on the trail.

This form of exercise had the great ability to raise one's spirits through the effects of endorphins, commonly referred to as "happy hormones" coursing in your body once you've done an exercise.

Every run completed, I felt lighter; it is like I could clear my mind of that fog of worry and doubt for a little while. Running helped me develop resilience-not just in physical endurance, but also in the way I tackled life. Just as I pushed through the pain and discomfort at the end of the last mile, so, too, was I able to overcome a difficult time in my life with that same determination.

As I started taking my runs a little more seriously, what stood out most in my mind was the ways in which exercise had developed a discipline and routine. Every morning run was a commitment I made to myself, a pledge to my well-being. It was an empowering experience-to know that my body and my mind were things I could control when so much around me seemed chaos. Of course, not every day was easy; on other days, it took a fight just to leave the bed. I found, though, that the most challenging part was always that first step out the door. Once I began, it became something I never regretted.

Aside from the endorphin high, exercise taught me about mental grit. Running was the mirror image of life in itself: like in life, there were always endless hills, plateaus where the energy level had been sapped, and moments when giving up was easier than carrying on. However, during every run, I learned to pace myself, be patient, and believe that eventually I would reach the finish line. These physical pains of running became metaphors for the struggles of life. When facing obstacles in daily life, I could draw from mental strengths built on the track. I knew I could endure more than I ever thought possible.

It also became an emotional outlet that allowed me time to go over in my mind what was bothering me with no judgment. In that moment of silence, I felt closer to my soul. I'd let my mind wander through memories, fears, hopes, and dreams, and many times returned a little wiser about life. Almost like therapy in motion, it was. I soon realized that through exercise-even as simple as a walk or jog-much healing can take place. Continuing to exercise only furthered my experiences beyond running into other forms of movement, like yoga, strength training, and even hiking. Each brought its unique value and sense of accomplishment. Yoga taught me the rewards of patience and slowing down. Strength training demonstrated what persistence and dedication could achieve. Hiking put me back in touch with nature, reminding me just how small the world is and I am within it.

Running and working out furthered this understanding by showing me that healing and growth are not quick fixes but ongoing practices which require time, patience, and consistency.

As much as the training of my body was needed, so was the training of the mind to approach life with endurance and resilience. With every run and every workout, I found that not only was I stronger than I had ever thought, more able was my body than I had ever imagined, but also I could do everything that came my way, on or off the track.

In this journey, what stands out most perhaps is that the care of our physical health is intertwined with mental well-being. Movement is medicine, and every step, every push, and every breath is a reminder that we are alive and capable of change. I hope that through my story, whoever reads this finds their own kind of movement-something that speaks to them and gives them a space to heal, grow, and reconnect with themselves.

Exercise and running did wonders for me, Remember when they told you to stay active and exercise in school to become healthy? They were right. Regular activity has numerous benefits for both mind and body. Particularly in combating negative self-perceptions. Exercise is a tool for enhancing self-esteem, resilience, and mental wellbeing, which enables individuals to overcoming detrimental self-thoughts.

It's scientifically proven that Physical activity stimulates the release of endorphins, also known as "feel-good" hormones, which improve mood and reduce stress levels. Exercise has been shown to decrease symptoms of anxiety and depression, fostering a more positive self-image. Moreover, achieving fitness goals and witnessing physical progress can significantly boost confidence.

Beyond the physiological effects, physical activity provides opportunities for social interaction and community engagement. Participating in team sports, group fitness classes, or simply exercising with friends can help individuals develop supportive networks, challenging negative self-talk and promoting a sense of belonging.

Furthermore, physical activity serves as a healthy distraction from harmful self-rumination. Focusing on physical accomplishments shifts attention away from self-criticism, cultivating self-compassion and self-awareness.

In conclusion, incorporating physical activity into daily life can profoundly impact mental health, empowering individuals to challenge and overcome negative self-perceptions. By harnessing the psychological benefits of exercise, we can cultivate a more positive, resilient self-image.

- **Releasing endorphins**: Exercise releases endorphins, which are brain chemicals that can improve your mood and sense of well-being.

- **Distracting you**: Exercise can take your mind off negative thoughts and worries. Every time I was at the gym it distracted my thoughts

- **Socializing**: Exercising with others can provide an opportunity to socialize and get social support

- **Reducing stress**: Exercise can help reduce stress and anxiety. It can also help your body practice working through the effects of stress, which can have positive effects on your body.

- **Increasing self-esteem**: Regular exercise can help increase your self-esteem. I never knew it could work but as soon as I started exercising I felt a huge bomb of confidence fall unto me and I became much more confident and secure in myself, & I felt good about myself too.

So exercise, you don't even need to do an hour, 20-30 minutes is more impactful than you think. And the best thing about it is there's no need to go to an expensive gym, you can train at the park, or buy your own equipment and train in the comfort of your own home.

How you should exercise:

Let's create a customized workout plan to help manage negative thoughts.

Your Goals:

1. Reduce stress and anxiety
2. Improve mood
3. Increase energy levels
4. Enhance focus and concentration

Your Preferences:

1. Exercise type (choose up to 2):
- Cardio (running, cycling, swimming)
- Strength training (weightlifting, bodyweight)
- Yoga or Pilates
- High-Intensity Interval Training (HIIT)
- Dance-based workouts

2. Exercise frequency:

- 3 times a week
- 4-5 times a week
- Daily

3. **Exercise duration:**

- 20-30 minutes
- 30-45 minutes
- 45-60 minutes

4. **Time of day:**

- Morning
- Afternoon
- Evening

5. Any physical limitations or health concerns?

Simple Workout Plan:

Monday (Cardio):*

1. Warm-up: 5-minute walk/jog
2. Brisk walking: 20 minutes
3. Cool-down: 5-minute stretching

Tuesday (Strength Training):

1. Squats: 3 sets of 10 reps
2. Lunges: 3 sets of 10 reps (per leg)
3. Push-ups: 3 sets of 10 reps
4. Cool-down: 5-minute stretching

Wednesday (Yoga):

1. Downward-facing dog: 30-second hold
2. Warrior II: 30-second hold (per leg)
3. Triangle pose: 30-second hold (per side)
4. Seated forward fold: 30-second hold

Thursday (HIIT):

1. Sprints: 30 seconds
2. Burgees: 30 seconds
3. Jump squats: 30 seconds
4. Rest for 30 seconds between exercises

Friday (Cardio):

1. Swimming: 20 minutes
2. Cycling: 20 minutes

Additional Tips:

1. Start with shorter sessions and gradually increase duration.
2. Incorporate mindfulness techniques during exercise.
3. Listen to uplifting music.
4. Find a workout buddy.
5. Reward yourself after reaching milestones.

PART 3

EMBRACING YOUR WORTH

'Healing takes time, and asking for help is a courageous step' – Robert Kiyosaki

Why It's Okay to Ask for Help

There's actually an important message we often don't catch in our fast-paced, self-sufficient world, and that is this: asking for help is not only okay, it's necessary. As human beings, we were never intended to go through life by ourselves. We are social creatures, wired for connection, and it's vital we remember that at times of struggle, confusion, or uncertainty. This is not only unrealistic but harmful-this idea that we should be able to handle it ourselves. By not reaching out for a hand, we deny ourselves access to the very support that will keep us prospering.

Most of us drag our feet when it comes to asking for help. We tell ourselves, "I don't want to burden anybody" or "I'll get through it by myself." It's a sense of reluctance that in some way stays in the back of one's mind, convincing a person that seeking help makes them weak or a burden. In reality, just the opposite is true. In fact, I can say now that those moments I did allow myself to reach out were the moments when I grew the most.

I lost nothing in those moments; quite the contrary, I received strength, clarity, and even an increase in connectedness with the people around me.

When we ask for help, we open the door to understanding. We open our doors to allow others to support us and show their care, which may give way to better relationships. Note that when someone helps us, it is not a one-way thing: just like we feel fulfilled in helping others, others feel the same sense of purpose when they can help us. It's mutually enriching-a beautiful balance strengthening the bonds we share.

Then why do we think others don't want to give the same in return? Why do we assume we must carry our burdens in silence and on our own?

The thing is, in asking for help, we're not just looking to be assisted; we're offering a gift-a gift of connection, a gift of trust. We are giving others an opportunity to become part of our journey-to share in our successes and our failures, and to know us a little bit deeper. It's this act of vulnerability-but also one of courage and self-awareness. If anything, asking for help is the recognition of our humanity: limitation and need, like everybody else.

Checking on our readiness to receive help is a necessary process in breaking the circle of self-reliance, sometimes destined to be lonely and overwhelming. There is nothing wrong with acknowledging that we are not in possession of all the answers. It is okay to need somebody to listen. The real strength, therefore, comes from recognizing that we are worthy of support, and that in seeking help we are not diminished, but actually enhanced, to go forward.

Reflection Prompt Converse with yourself concerning an area of your life in which you've been feeling struggling on work, relationships, or personal growth, or whatever other type of challenge is present. Now, picture having to share it with someone who really cares about you. Visualize their response: What might they say to encourage you? And how do you think they could help you look at it from a different perspective or provide the support you need?

This might be quite a powerful way to start perceiving asking for help as an opportunity, not a burden: write down your thoughts and imagine this exchange.

Engagement

"I am deserving of support, and it is okay for me to ask for help. Reaching out is not a sign of weakness but, rather, proof of my strength and my trust in others."

No one has to navigate the challenges of life in isolation. We are interconnected, and we each can offer something to someone else. A request for help is an opportunity to be seen, heard, and supported. The more we lean into this truth, the more we will create with one another a community of care and understanding that will elevate us all. So whenever you are facing any challenge, do not hesitate to reach out because you will never be alone

Breaking Down the Stigma of Asking for Help

To so many of us, the very notion of asking for help carries with it one stigma-a rather condescending idea that somehow it makes us "less than." So often in our experience, we fear that with an admission of needing support comes a signal of weakness, incompetence, or worst of all, that we are a burden to the people around us. But the reality is that to ask for help is not a sign of weakness; asking for help is one of the bravest and most powerful things we can do. It requires vulnerability and trust and readiness to acknowledge our humanness that we are human and need the contact with another. It is often in asking for help that we find our greatest strength.

The stigma runs deep for getting help, influenced a lot by cultural and societal beliefs. In some cultures, mental health is taboo, and therefore not to be discussed. In others, there exists a social expectation of hiding one's struggles-often the unspoken rule is that only the "strong" can handle life's challenges alone.

We are often taught that strong people are self-sufficient, that they "deal with it" in private. But this myth is unsafe: it not only makes us isolated but also justifies continuing the culture of shame and silence, further exacerbating our struggles.

On the bright side, the world is indeed changing, little by little. More and more voices speak up about taking care of one's mental health and shed light on seeking help. Public figures, celebrities, and people just like you are tearing down the barriers that once restrained them from exposing their vulnerabilities. In sharing their stories, they show that asking for help is okay-it's okay not to have all of the answers. This shift in the cultural narrative of what is correct and appropriate is making allowance for space, allowance for understanding that strength does not come from silence but from our efforts to reach out and connect and be supported.

Essentially, when we ask for help, we open ourselves to growth, healing, and deeper connections with others. It is the acknowledgment that we are worthy of care, that we deserve to be seen and heard and supported in times of need. This, per se, is not a sign of failure but a reflection of our commitment to living authentically-to taking care of ourselves and embracing the journey of self-improvement.

And in doing so, by breaking down these barriers and changing this narrative on asking for help, we create a far more compassionate world: one where vulnerability is celebrated and seeking support is an act of strength, not of weakness. By reframing how we view asking for help ourselves, we can encourage others to do the same-a ripple effect that empowers us all to show up as our true selves, unafraid to seek and offer support.

Reflection Prompt

Take a moment and write down your biggest fear about asking for help. What holds you back from reaching out? Once you have identified this fear, challenge it - reframe it. For example, take the fear that "If I ask for help, people will think I'm weak." Reframed, it would sound something like this: "When I ask for help, I show my strength and commitment to growth." We should challenge those fears so that the shift in our thinking becomes healthier and more supportive.

Key Takeaway

Seeking help is a brave decision: it means I'm ready to live life authentically and take good care of myself. It is an act of strength, not of weakness.

Understanding the Need to Speak Up

In most of us, there's this prevailing belief that keeping quiet is the "strong" thing to do. We say things to ourselves like, "I don't want to burden anyone" or "People have their own problems to deal with." The roots of such thoughts are often laid in our noble desire to protect others from the pain we have to bear, but what we fail to realize is that, in so many ways, silence is even heavier than speaking up. Every time we bottle up our feelings, we are putting one more invisible weight inside our soul. And the more we suppress our struggles, the larger, heavier, and more consuming they get to carry.

Speaking up is not about asking others to take our burdens away from us; it is an opportunity given unto ourselves to lighten the weight we carry. That means taking responsibility for what one is feeling, the weight of it he or she carries, and permission to be heard. This speaking out is not an act of weakness; on the contrary, it's a powerful act that articulates self-respect and courage. We often believe that silence is a form of strength, but in actuality, silence is merely stagnation in forms. Silence can keep us under the water, barely paddling to try and stay afloat among thoughts and emotions. It's only when we finally break that silence, opening up, that we allow ourselves to breathe again.

LOVE,

ME

I can remember how long it took me to realize it is important to speak up. Throughout years, I thought that if I kept my struggles inside, they would eventually go away or fix themselves. And they never did; they just intensified. The longer it took me to say something, the more unbearable it was.

My concerns mounted, my thoughts weighing me down even further. Only when I started to talk about what happened to me, sharing with my loved ones, did I start to feel those burdens lighten just a little. Often, it wasn't even about finding advice or solutions. Simply saying, "I'm not okay," had been enough to bring a sense of relief-just vocalizing my struggles was often enough as the pressure loosened.

Think of it like trying to breathe underwater: in silence, it's as if we are submerged in our own pain, straining for a breath. We're quickly overwhelmed by that pressure, smothered under the weight of our own thoughts. It is like that breakthrough through the water's surface, when we find our voice, taking that necessary breath of fresh air and feeling our lungs expand with relief. It is in speaking that there is a release-a moment of letting go-of allowing oneself to be free from the weight that holds one down.

It is so easy to be of the belief that when we speak up, this will only burden others, but actually quite the opposite is true, especially in most cases: people who are on our important list are waiting for us to reach out. They want to be there for us, not out of obligation, but because they simply care and want to ease our pain. Speaking up opens the door to connection and support. It gives way to deeper relationships and reminds us that we don't have to go through life's struggles all by ourselves.

The more we speak out, the more we empower ourselves to take our lives into our own hands. We get our peace back. We get our power back. We remind ourselves that our voice should be heard, that our struggles are real, and that our voices count.

It is sharing that frees us, and it is sharing that creates space for others. For a culture of openness, for support- it is safe to be vulnerable and candid about your experiences.

Reflection Prompt

Now think of a difficulty you had recently with which you did not share your feelings. How did keeping quiet affect your mood or energy afterward? Did it make you feel alone? Did it deplete your emotional reserves? Now, imagine what might have happened if you confided in a trusted friend or loved one. How do you think that would have shifted your perspective, or how you felt in that moment?

Takeaway Key "I deserve to be heard, and speaking up means I take control of my life and my peace. My voice matters, and sharing my struggles lightens the load and opens up a space for the support that I deserve.

Embracing Vulnerability as Strength

There's something so deeply metamorphic in really coming to understand that vulnerability is not indicative of weakness but really a path to true strength. Long, we have been socialized to understand that strength is all about being stoic, masking our emotions, and dealing with our struggles alone.

We are socialized to be tough: to keep quiet, to push our feelings deep inside, and to carry our crosses alone. But in reality, strength is not in keeping silent but rather in the act of being able to say, "I need help." It emanates from being brave enough to show our true selves-flaws, scars, and all-and trusting that by doing so, we find healing, support, and connection.

Let's imagine for one moment carrying all that weight day in and day out, being alone. That is very exhausting, both physically and emotionally. The weight does not get any lighter; with every passing day, it gets even heavier to carry.

Our minds are filled with turmoil, our heart is loaded, and the energy is sapped dry. But in reaching out and finding strength to say, "This is too much for me right now," that is a step toward freedom. We give ourselves permission to be human-to feel, be raw, vulnerable, and imperfect. And it is in that moment of vulnerability that we let go of the death grip on the burden we have carried for so long.

Speaking up, seeking help, and opening to others are all acts of courage. It's here that we begin again to breathe; it is here that we allow ourselves space to heal, grow. Every time we speak our truth, we take away a layer of the weight we have been carrying. Of course, it won't happen overnight. It would be gradual, accomplished word by word, step by step toward vulnerability. It's a way of reaching out-not weakness, but resilience. It takes an awful lot of strength to be open and to allow others glimpses of those hidden parts of ourselves that we have spent so many years concealing. It is in those moments of vulnerability that our deepest strength finds its origin.

Vulnerability-all through my journey-is a bridge to healing, I have come to understand. In fact, there came a time in my life when I kept everything inside, bottling it up in my head and thinking that somehow, if I just managed to hold it all together, it would be fine. I thought that so long as I held up a good front, nothing was ever going to be able to touch me. The fact was, I wasn't okay. I was breaking under the burden of everything inside of me. The longer I was silent, the heavier it got. It was only when I started voicing up, sharing my struggles with close friends and loved ones, that I started feeling peace, which I didn't know existed.

It felt like I had been wearing this mask for years, and when I let it fall, I could breathe again. That's when I realized vulnerability wasn't something to be avoided but rather welcomed. My truth, spoken, brought healing not only to me but also allowed me to connect with the people around me on a much deeper level.

Vulnerability isn't about being weak; it's about being human. It is in acknowledging our needs, our fears, and our pain without shame. It is trusting we are worthy of support, that our struggles are valid, and sharing them can get us to a place of healing. In those moments when we allow ourselves to be vulnerable, we open the door to transformation. We open ourselves to the present moment, in which no hiding or pretending is any longer necessary. We permit ourselves to be whole, to be real, and to pursue healing because of this.

Reflection Prompt

Consider times when you felt so vulnerable that you were scared to let anyone see it. What held you back from opening up to? What held you back from telling others of your struggles? What fears or beliefs did you have? Write down those fears now and reflect on them. Imagine what could have happened if you had opened yourself to others. How might you have felt differently, and what kind of support or understanding could you have gained?

Takeaway Affirmation

Vulnerability is my strength. I am brave enough to share my experiences, fully aware that with each sharing, I am brought closer to my healing and the connections that will see me grow. I believe that embracing my vulnerability is a strong step toward my becoming.

The Magic of Letting Go

Illustrated by Fiona Montanez

Letting go is perhaps one of the most difficult, yet transformative, things we can ever do. It is somewhat paradoxical, really, as we often hold on tight to what hurts and what we fear losing in an attempt to find control if we can only grip tighter. But the more we are holding on to, the heavier it gets until we are consumed by the very thing we are trying to avoid. The weight of it bears down upon us, and yet we are Scotch-taping our fingers together, refusing to let go. Letting go isn't about giving up; it's about recognizing much of this is outside of our control. It is about choosing peace over pain, freedom over fear.

There's something deeply ingrained within our culture that says holding on makes us strong. We have been socialized to believe that to let go is to surrender, that when we stop fighting is when we will surely lose. However, true strength lies not in clinging onto things not meant for us but in recognizing when it is time to release, to step back, and allow life to take its natural course. Letting go isn't weakness, but wisdom.

It's just a testimony that, no matter how much we fight some battles, quite frankly, aren't ours to win.

I remember so well having to learn this and struggling deeply with it. I thought that if I kept pushing, just kept trying to "fix" everything, I could control the outcome. Well, I felt that if I could work hard enough, stay strong enough, I would be able to mend the broken parts of my life, fill the emptiness, or heal the wounds. I thought I had to make everything right: in relationships, in career, or even within myself. But what I learned after all those frustrating and painful years was that sometimes the most courageous thing we can do is simply to let go.

Indeed, letting go of people, situations, and beliefs that no longer serve us is terribly hard; it is a prerequisite for growth. We aren't even aware of this, but we hang on to things because we're scared of the unknown. We fear that if we let go, we will fall apart, or what comes next won't be as good as it is now. By holding on, however, we block new opportunities, experiences, and joys that could come into our life. Think of how much we cling to these expectations, either of our own making or instilled within us by others. Basically, the fear of disappointment-to others, to a perfect image of ourselves-can totally paralyze us. I lived for years with a low-grade undercurrent of pressure-the need to be perfect, to live up to the expectations of others, to succeed in ways that looked good on paper. But the more I tried to meet those expectations, the more I lost myself in the process.

So focused on what I thought I should be doing, I didn't take the time to ask myself what I wanted to do-or what actually would make me happy. And in that fight, I realized something much more crucial: we are not defined by what we can control or by the way we can meet other people's expectations. We are defined by how we can let go of what doesn't resonate with our soul.

Letting go is not giving up; it's an act of acceptance. It is learning to accept that some things are quite beyond our control and simply to trust that life will unfold in its right time. Not every outcome in life can be forced, nor should we try. What's meant for us sometimes comes, while what is not meant will leave. We don't have to hold on to everything. But essentially, to let go is to release space-space for something new, something better, an opportunity to be more congruent with who we really are and are growing into.

There's a deep freedom in release. For the first time, perhaps in a very long time, we breathe. Unencumbered by the weight of expectation, resentment, or fear of failure, lighter, more open to possibilities.

A release of pressure that invites us to reconnect with ourselves and the world at deeper levels than ever before.

But that's not easy: to let go is a process in time. We may need to let go more than once-of people, of beliefs, of dreams that no longer serve us. We may even need to let go of parts of ourselves that we once thought were integral to who we are. And that's okay. We grow by letting go-by shedding the layers that no longer fit who we are becoming.

What I have learned is that growth is absolutely not linear. It, in essence, doesn't fall on a specific path and does not necessarily look like what we often expect. Sometimes, for growth to occur, it means releasing those things that we never thought would be possible. The relationships we thought would last a lifetime, the job that at one point brought us so much joy but is now viewed as sucking the life out of us, the mind-set which once served us but is keeping us small now-letting go of these things is incredibly difficult, but often it's the very thing that allows us to move forward.

Think of it like this: if you have a handful of sand, no matter how tight you clench it, it's going slide through your fingers. The tighter you hold it, the more it gets away.

But when you relax your grip, when you open your hand, the sand is still in the palm. Letting go is never about losing; it is about creating a void where something new can come in, new relations can get formed, and new opportunities can come your way. But when we let go, we are sacrificing nothing. What we do is make room for something better, which is in accordance with our purpose.

Letting go can be a path to peace. Releasing the need to control frees one from the constant anxiety seeking to make everything right. When we let go of the need when we stop looking to others for our approval, we can stand in our own power and know that, as we are, we are enough. Peace is not found in external circumstances, nor in what we cling to; instead, may it be found in our capacity to let go, to trust, and to let life happen.

Letting go doesn't mean abandoning everything or letting go of the dream. It simply means knowing when to hold on to what is healthy and when to let go of what gets in the way. It's time to realize what really saps your energy and be able to hold onto what replenishes your spirit. It means being discriminative and choosing what will nourish you.

So what does it look like to let go? It's different for everyone.

For some, this might mean the end of a relationship that no longer serves them. For others, it could mean leaving behind a career that has grown unfulfilling. It might mean releasing old beliefs about ourselves that have held us back for years. That could be as simple as releasing the guilt we harbour for things we cannot control. Whatever it is, it's about finding the courage to let go of what no longer contributes to your peace and happiness.

Letting go is not an event; it is a continuous practice-a choice we make each day, a releasing of the need to control and an act of faith in the unfolding process. And each time we let go, we create more space for growth, for healing, and peace-so wished for. Reflection Prompt:

Now bring to mind something you are holding onto out of fear-something in a relationship, a belief, or an expectation of yourself. What would that be like, to let go of this burden? How might it make room for something new and improved in its place? Take some time to journal about the feelings you have surrounding holding on, and how letting go might change your life. What could you possibly gain from releasing this fear or attachment?

Takeaway Affirmation:

"I release what no longer serves me, trusting that letting go opens space for my growth and healing. I trust the process of life; it's unfolding everything for my highest good. I am ready to receive and welcome whatever new opportunities may come as a result of letting go of the past and stepping into my power."

Never change yourself to fit in somewhere you don't belong

Standing Alone

There are those moments in life when one finds themselves standing alone-no one beside them, no hand to hold. It is terrorizing, being cast away in some wide-open space where the tautological silence presses from every side. One may feel forsaken, frail, and even unworthy of the space occupied. The world often screams at us that to be somebody, we need people around us to feel validation, support, and approval to complete us. But in that silence of standing alone lies a quiet power that most of the world would rather not see. It is the power within. It's a force, standing in yourself amidst all the surrounding prejudices or misunderstandings.

Standing alone doesn't mean abandoned; it means standing into your truth. We are refusing to bend, to compromise, or apologize for the person that we are. This is not a position of weakness but one of strength. It means embracing solitude and trusting that in this quiet, we are becoming exactly who we are supposed to be. We don't need the validation of another person to tell us we are adequate. We are complete, worthy, and capable. The courage to stand alone is the courage of being true and uncompromisingly ourselves against doubt or uncertainty.

Approval Wars

Since we were little, our lives are shaped by how we need to seek approval to succeed. We adjust ourselves by fitting into the mould of what society or our families expect from us. From grades to circles, from the way we dress to how we speak, we get conditioned to get people's approval for feeling valuable.

This need for approval is instilled within us; we were taught that to belong is the ultimate goal. But what happens when we actually do not seek that external validation anymore and start to stand firm on our own values, our own beliefs, and our own self-worth?

The shift is subtle yet powerful: We begin to realize that in this and every moment, we are enough-beyond anyone's approval to make us worthy. We no longer link our self-worth to the opinion of others. Instead, we build up the courage to trust ourselves and take our path, even when this sets us apart from the crowd. This shift does not always come easily; it generally means having to let go of the need for likable and accepted feelings by all people. But it frees.

The truth is, the only approval we really need is our own. It is when we stop looking for validation from the world around us that we begin to stand tall on our own. We learn to value our own judgment and decisions over the noise of the external world. This strength doesn't come overnight; it's earned through countless small moments of standing up for ourselves, of choosing to listen to our own voice, and of embracing the solitude that comes with being true to ourselves.

The Solitude That Strengthens

I have had to learn most of my life to stand alone. This is a lesson I have never embraced but which has so far turned me into someone stronger than I could have ever believed: misunderstood, isolated, and unsupported; fighting battles, it seemed, that none else could either see or understand. These feelings of loneliness made me sometimes wish that someone would just appear and say everything would be okay, that I was not the only one having these struggles.

What I didn't understand at that time was that the moments of solitude carry with them the greatest strength. It is in those quiet times that we find out who we really are. We realize that we can stand firm on our own. We do not need the approval of any other person to feel worthy of love, success, or happiness. All that is required is our approval. And once we give ourselves that approval, everything changes.

Standing alone is not a weakness; it simply means we are strong enough to stand up for our thoughts without distraction, with no validation needed from anyone else. It is in those quiet times, when no one is looking at us, that we find the deepest parts of ourselves. It is then that we grow most. When we stop searching others for support, we begin trusting in ourselves. We will learn that we can get through anything with grace and resilience, be that with someone standing beside us or not.

There is, of course, a certain strength in embracing solitude: self-sufficiency, a quiet inner strength. It is when we stand alone that we learn to listen to our own voice, to trust our own decisions, to find peace in our own company. That's where the growth truly happens. We realize to feel intact, we don't have to have people around us; we are already whole. Standing Alone Lessons

Each time I had to stand alone, there was something new about myself which I would end up learning. And then there came a time when the world really seemed to be against me and only I was fighting for my cause. I felt lost, but the more I embraced my solitude, the more I began to see that my strength didn't come from external validation; it was derived from my belief in myself.

I recall a time in my life when a decision had to be made that ran against the grain of what was expected of me. It was one of those decisions that left me isolated, not supported by anyone in my surroundings. In the beginning, I felt defeated-like I'd made a mistake in choosing a path no one around understood. But with time, I realized it's the guts to stand alone which actually gave me strength for making the right decision. The more I learn to trust myself, the more my path may be at times lonely, but it will be a path that will truly satiate me.

Standing alone does not mean we must do it forever. We don't have to live in isolation, cut off from others. But at times, we must stand alone so as to hear our own voice, to clarify our own direction. It is during those moments that we learn to trust in our own abilities to handle anything that comes before us. The courage to be alone is the kind of courage it takes to choose ourselves, to put our well-being above everything else, and to trust that with time, we shall find our way.

Reflection Prompt:

Now reflect back to a time when you felt isolated or perhaps lonely. How did you manage? What perception into your inner resilience did you have in those moments? How can you apply the same resilience at this time? Reflect on how being alone allowed for growth and how much more deeply you were able to look within yourself for your own sense of security. Write about any ways in which you might embrace loneliness as an ally.

Takeaway Affirmation:

I am strong, even in solitude. I believe in myself to handle life with graciousness and strength. I am enough as I am, and

I give myself the permission to stand into my truth unapologetically and fearlessly. I trust myself, and in that trust, I find my true strength.

Eventually, being braver than anyone else means trusting ourselves and being our own biggest ally, knowing that we do not need any other person's unsolicited approval of whether we shall succeed, be loved, or be happy. That is a lesson to be learned by each and every one of us, yet one that eventually will make us stronger, more resilient, and confident in the person we become.

PART 4

MAINTAINING MOMENTUM

'Never confuse motion with action.'

– Benjamin Franklin

Redefining Success

Success. It is a word that carries such a load in our society, having been heavily created by external factors: wealth, status, achievements, and accolades. We grow up hearing from everyone around us that it is something we must pursue; it is about achieving milestones, collecting things, and gaining approval. We pursue these markers, really believing they'll translate to lives that will in some way make us feel meaningful, purpose-driven, and fulfilled.

What if we've been trying to use the wrong yardstick to measure success? What if it was true that success is not what we achieve on the outside, but how we feel about ourselves and the world along the way?

What if it is within the journey and not the destination that success can be found-in times of peace, small acts of kindness, quiet victories, and the courage to keep going when everything else seems to fall apart?

Well, for the greater part of my life, I too defined success by external markers. Success, I thought, had to do with reaching certain milestones, getting a promotion or penning some bestseller or making just enough money to live comfortably. I actually thought when I achieved these things, I'll finally feel fulfilled, as if these external markers somehow held the keys to happiness. But what I actually came to realize is that every time I reached one of those goals, I was left feeling empty. The achievement itself never gave me the fulfilment I had thought it would. What I was really hungering for wasn't the achievement-it was the acknowledgment that came along with it. I need to feel seen, appreciated, and worthy.

It wasn't until I stopped measuring my value by outside metrics that I started to understand what true success actually looked like. I realized along the way that success doesn't reside in the shiny trophies or accolades we accumulate. It doesn't dwell in the number of zeroes on a pay check or the prestige of a job title. True success is found in the quiet, intimate moments-the times when we make a conscious effort to show up for ourselves and for others. It's an inside job, not just an outside achievement. It's about how we treat ourselves, how we accept ourselves, blemishes and all, and learn to live contented with who we are rather than trying to be something or another person's version of success.

That wasn't an easy realization. First, I had to unlearn a lot of the conditioning on what success is. I had to let go of this notion that success is something which we earn, it's a measuring outcome, and move into the belief that, in fact, success is what we cultivate: personal growth, kindness, resilience. It's in how we show up every day despite the obstacles, despite the doubts. Success resides in courage-the courage to keep moving ahead, even when the way forward is not clear. It is in recognizing and rejoicing in small victories-the quiet wins that may not make headlines but that carry more weight in our hearts.

Gradually, I began to realize that success is not a place; it's a process. It is opting to release pressure, embracing growth and self-acceptance instead of perfection and other people's validation. Success is the ability to look in the mirror and say, "I am enough," even though every external goal we may have set for ourselves is not accomplished. That's about recognizing our worth is not dictated by what we do but by who we are-persons of integrity, kindness, resilience, and growth through life's challenges.

LOVE,

ME

Shifting the Focus to Internal Growth

As I started to move my focus away from accomplishing external feats to growing internally, I started to feel a deep sense of peace and fulfilment in my life. I stopped pursuing a version of success that wasn't mine and began nurturing a life that reflected my values and passions. The more I operated within this new definition of success,

The more fun and meaning I found there was in process, not just outcome. It's a process.

For example, setbacks were no longer setbacks or failures. Rather, I began to see them as opportunities for growth, opportunities to learn more about myself, refine my strengths, and further develop new skills.

Success started to come into view: learning from my mistakes, taking the time to be patient with myself when times were rough, finding moments of gratitude for those instants of quiet and peace. I began to understand that I didn't have to have it all figured out to be successful. In fact, the capacity to Embrace the uncertainty and let go of the need to control was in itself an action of success.

This shift in perspective has changed how I approach life's challenges. Instead of stressing over how my achievements will be perceived by others, I focus on the satisfaction that comes from doing my best and staying true to my values. I no longer chase after success as if it's a prize to be won; instead, I embrace it as a natural by-product of living authentically, taking care of my well-being, and nurturing the relationships that matter most to me.

Remember to Breathe, relax, and trust the process.

The Power of Small Moments

In my journey toward redefining success, I've come to realize that success is often hidden in the small moments—the quiet, everyday acts of kindness, compassion, and self-care that can easily be overlooked. Success is the ability to wake up each day and choose to show up for yourself, no matter how difficult life may feel. It's in the simple act of being present with the people you love, offering a listening ear to a friend, or showing compassion to someone who's struggling. These small, seemingly insignificant moments are often the most meaningful, and they are where true success can be found.

Success isn't about having everything figured out or always being the best. It's about making progress, however small, toward becoming the person you want to be. It's about the courage to continue moving forward, even when things don't go according to plan. It's about knowing that your value isn't tied to the results of your actions, but to the effort you put in and the love you give.

True success is about embracing the imperfections of life, and finding beauty in the messiness of our human experience.

Reflection Prompt:

Take a moment to reflect on how you define success. What external markers have you been chasing? How might redefining success, focusing on internal growth and peace, change the way you approach life's challenges? How might it impact your sense of self-worth and happiness? Consider what success looks like for you now, and how you can create a life that aligns with your new definition.

Takeaway Affirmation:

"I define success on my own terms. True success is found in peace, growth, and self-acceptance, not in external achievements. I embrace my journey, knowing that every step, no matter how small, is a part of my unique path. I am enough, and I choose to find success in the way I live, love, and grow."

Redefining success is an ongoing process—a continual shifting of perspective that allows us to live more authentically and with greater peace.

When we begin to understand that success is not about what we achieve or accumulate, but about how we show up for ourselves and others, we free ourselves from the pressure of external expectations. Success, in its truest form, is about living a life that reflects our inner truth, our values, and our purpose. It's about creating a life that feels fulfilling, not because of what we have, but because of who we are. This shift in perspective has since changed my attitude toward the trials of life. I do not concern myself with how well others would perceive my success but find great satisfaction in doing well and staying true to myself. Success isn't something that I pursue as if it's a trophy; it is the positive side-effect of an authentic life in which one takes care of oneself and nourishes the meaningful relationships in one's life.

Whatever you do, trust in God

The Power of Small Moments

Success for me has become the sum of the little moments: quiet, unassuming acts of kindness, compassion, and self-care that go largely unnoticed. It's the act of rising every day with the capability and strength to make a choice for yourself-to show up.

It's in the simple act of being present with people you love, being able to lend a listening ear to a friend, or showing compassion to someone who's struggling. These small and often insignificant-seeming moments are often the most meaningful, and they are places of true success.

Success doesn't mean having all the answers or always being the best. It's about the small steps toward becoming a person you want to be. It is about the courage to keep moving forward, it is about realizing your worth doesn't eliminate from the results of an action you take, but rather in the effort placed in and the love given. Success, in fact, embraces all of the imperfections of life and finds the unruly, chaotic aspects of human experience to be beautiful.

Reflection Prompt:

Take a moment to reflect on how you define success. What external markers have you been chasing?

How might this redefinition of success, focusing on internal growth and peace, alter the way you approach the challenges in your life? How might it affect your self-worth and happiness? Consider what success is for you now and how you can build a life that reflects your new definition.

Takeaway Affirmation:

I define success in my terms. True success is to be found in peace, growth, and self-acceptance, not to be found in external achievements. I love my journey; every step, no matter how small, is part of a road that is mine alone. Enough I am, and I choose to find success in the way I live, love, and grow.

Success is a process-a constantly changing perspective through which we learn to live more authentically. And we start to see that, if truth be told, success is not what we accomplish or gain; rather, it is how we show up to our life and others. Then, we release the need for external expectations. Success, in its real sense, is living a life that expresses the inner truth, values, and purpose of an individual. It is the creation of a life that feels complete, not because of what one possesses but because of whom one is.

You will never be happy when you rich & you will never be rich when you happy, what does this mean? I'm not talking about being rich financially, I am talking about being rich emotionally, that's where success starts if you not emotionally rich you will only make irrational decisions and choices that will only dig your own grave.

This means that success starts from within, it starts from what you feeling in the inside, in order to start taking control of your life you have to face the demons inside including the pain you hiding because keeping these stored inside will only lead you to making irrational decisions. I made these irrational decisions by ruining important relationships in my life, so don't do the same. Have you ever heard of the expression that "you can't love someone else until you love yourself", I had to learn that it's true, I ruined most of my relationships because of the negative way I was living which was affecting these relationships in the process

What God has for you cannot be stolen or lost

Here's an ugly drawing that I did, a drawing of Gary, Gary lost his leg in a traumatic experience & he wishes he could fit in with the other kids but they have made it so hard for him because they make fun of him which leads him to have all these negative thoughts and doubts of himself and these thoughts are filled in his brain.

See how the mind works? Everything around us dictates how we move whether we like to hear that or not, Gary never wished to lose his leg, no one would too, but because life throws dreadful things on our way he got into a traumatic accident which made him have a hard time connecting with people even though he wants to, not only that but after the accident the people around him made it even more hard because they looked down on him and made fun of him.

Now someone with Gary's disability, he can't bring his leg back even if he wanted to it just won't be the same which makes him have a low self -esteem and a hard time connecting with people because he knows that they will think he is weird. We need to learn to be kind, when we show kindness to others, it not only improves their day but also boosts our own mood & sense of purpose. Research has shown that acts of kindness release endorphins, also known as "feel-good" hormones, which enhance our physical and mental health.

Breaking down Barriers

Kindness transcends cultural, social, and economic boundaries. It speaks a universal language that everyone understands, regardless of background or circumstances. By being kind, we bridge gaps, and foster empathy, helping to break down stereotypes and prejudice.

Creating a Ripple effect

Kindness has a ripple effect, inspiring others to pay it forward. One act of kindness can spark a chain reaction, spreading positive and compassion, throughout a community.

Cultivating Empathy

Kindness cultivates empathy, allowing us to see things from another person's perspective. This understanding helps to build stronger, more meaningful relationships and resolve conflicts peacefully.

Conclusion

In conclusion, kindness is a powerful tool that can bring people together, improve mental and physical health, and create a more harmonious world. By incorporating kindness into our daily lives, we can make a significant difference and inspire others to do the same.

As Mahatma Gandhi once said, "Be the change you wish to see in the world". Let us strive to be that change by spreading kindness wherever we go.

Words of affirmation to kick start your day:

Morning affirmations:

1. Today is a new day, full of new opportunities
2. I wake up with purpose and intention
3. I am enough, exactly as I am
4. I trust myself & my abilities
5. I am strong, resilient, and capable

Confidence boosters:

1. I am worthy of love, respect, and happiness
2. My thoughts are positive, my actions are intentional
3. I believe in myself and my dreams
4. I am beautiful inside and out
5. I am deserving of success and achievement

Gratitude & Positivity

1. I am grateful for another day to live, learn & grow.
2. I choose to focus on the good in every situation
3. I am surrounded by abundance and possibility
4. I trust that everything will work out in the end
5. I am filled with joy, love and positivity

How to use these affirmations

1. Repeat them aloud with conviction
2. Write them down in your journal
3. Set reminders on your phone
4. Create a vision board with inspiring images.
5. Share with a friend or accountability partner.

Overcoming Obstacles:

The obstacles we go through in life are hard but maybe they are necessary, I do wish I never let the negative noise inside as a kid, but now today I can stand and say that "I am grateful I went through the hard challenges because they made me stronger, but this can only apply if you use the pain in a purposeful way instead of drowning with yourself or feeling sorry for yourself, I had to use these challenges as fuel, How do we overcome these obstacles? We overcome them by not allowing them to control us, we use the pain to help us become better humans, this doesn't only apply to people who grew up with negativity around them, and this also applies to people who've gone through a breakup, loss & grief.

Strategies of dealing with setbacks:

Here are some strategies for dealing with setbacks and criticism:

Dealing with Setbacks:

1. Acknowledge and accept emotions: Recognize and validate your feelings.
2. Reframe perspective: View setbacks as opportunities for growth.
3. Identify lessons learned: Reflect on what went wrong and how to improve.
4. Develop a growth mind set: Focus on progress, not perfection.
5. Create a contingency plan: Prepare for potential future setbacks.
6. Seek support: Reach out to trusted friends, family, or mentors.
7. Practice self-care: Take care of physical and emotional well-being.
8. Focus on the present: Don't dwell on past setbacks or worry about future ones.

Dealing with Criticism:

1. Stay calm and composed: Manage emotions to respond constructively.
2. Listen actively: Understand the critic's perspective.
3. Separate feedback from criticism: Focus on constructive feedback.
4. Avoid defensiveness: Recognize valid points and learn from them.
5. Practice self-compassion: Treat yourself with kindness.
6. Seek clarification: Ask questions to understand critic's intent.

7. Develop a thick skin: Learn to handle criticism graciously.

8. Focus on solutions: Use criticism as an opportunity for growth.

Resilience-Building Strategies:

1. Develop a positive self-image: Cultivate self-confidence.

2. Build a support network: Surround yourself with positive influences.

3. Practice mindfulness: Stay present and focused.

4. Develop problem-solving skills: Approach challenges with a growth mind set.

5. Learn from failures: View failures as opportunities for growth.

6. Cultivate gratitude: Focus on positive aspects.

7. Practice self-care: Prioritize physical and emotional well-being.

8. Develop a growth mind set: Embrace challenges and learning.

Criticism Response Template:

1. Acknowledge: "Thank you for sharing your concerns."

2. Clarify: "Can you elaborate on what you mean by...?"

3. Reflect: "I understand your perspective."

4. Learn: "What can I improve on?"

5. Respond: "Here's my plan to address the issue."

Creating a support network & Building positive relationships:

Building positive & longer lasting relationships is a crucial step in overcoming negativity because having people who can be a backbone of support uplifted me to keep going, the support of my family was a huge impact and I don't think I would've got through the tunnel without them, whenever I felt negative about myself I'd go and spend time with my sister as a distraction and it gave me a bit of light and positivity, all you have to do is ask "how are you?', 'how was your day?" and if you do this with the people you around you will not only open room for relationships but a support system that will reciprocate the positive energy you giving them. I am not much of a social person, I'm quite introverted actually but the comes a time in life when you have to be outside your comfort zone because that's where growth happens, we all have to talk to people in our everyday lives whether we like it or not. We all need people in our lives but you have to make sure that the people you spend your time with are motivated, driven, uplifting, & want only what's best for you in order to become the best version of yourself we need support and then we reciprocate the same energy towards these people. "show me your friends and I will show you your future", this quote resonates with me in a far deeper level because although I had a few good friends in the past, most of them were full of negativity and bad influencers in which I consumed the energy the more time I spent with them until I enabled myself to say "no, I need more positive people in my life."

We need to be able to tell the difference between what's good for us and what's bad, noticing these differences with a plan/vision for your life and being courageous enough to walk away from the negativity, then you can open room for more healthier lasting relationships.

Why a Support Network is Crucial:

1. Emotional support: Helps cope with negative emotions.
2. Practical help: Assists with daily tasks and responsibilities.
3. Positive influence: Surrounds you with uplifting people.
4. Diverse perspectives: Offers new insights and solutions.

Identifying Potential Support Network Members:

1. Friends: Trusted, empathetic, and supportive.
2. Family: Loving, understanding, and encouraging.
3. Mentors: Experienced, wise, and guiding.
4. Therapists: Professional, objective, and skilled.
5. Support Groups: Shared experiences, understanding, and community.
6. Online Communities: Forums, social media groups, and online support groups.

Building Your Support Network:

1. Reach out to existing relationships.
2. Attend social events, join clubs or groups.
3. Volunteer, participate in community activities.
4. Join online communities and forums.
5. Connect with mentors, coaches, or industry experts.

Effective Communication Strategies:

1. Active listening: Engage fully with others.
2. Open communication: Share thoughts, feelings, and concerns.

3. Set boundaries: Prioritize self-care and emotional well-being.

4. Show appreciation: Express gratitude to network members.

Support Network Categories:

1. Emotional Support: friends, family, therapist.
2. Practical Support: colleagues, mentors, helpers.
3. Professional Support: coaches, advisors, industry experts.

Tips for Maintaining a Support Network:

1. Regular check-ins: Stay connected and updated.
2. be proactive: Don't wait for others to reach out.
3. Show appreciation: Express gratitude and value network members.
4. Respect boundaries: Prioritize self-care and emotional well-being.

Overcoming Negativity with Your Support Network:

1. Share concerns and feelings.
2. Seek advice and guidance.
3. Practice positive reframing.
4. Engage in activities promoting positivity.
5. Celebrate successes and progress.

LOVE,

ME

Self-reflection and Growth

Why self-reflection is important?

Self-reflection is what you define it, for me it means taking a moment of deep breathing, realizing that I've made it to the other side of the tunnel no matter how difficult it was, then I try to see if I'm still the same person that I was a few months ago, has there been positive changes and am I proud of the person I am now.

Illustration by Fiona Montanez

This is an important part of my journey because it pushed me to make even the tiniest bit of changes in my life mentally and physically because I knew that later on I am going to look back and self-reflect. It does not matter how much big of a change you make, what matters is the 1% of change every day which will shape you into a much better version that I assure you will be proud of. All our influences and heroes make these changes every day in their lives to become the people we see on social media. None of these changes are easy in-fact these small changes are quite hard. Let's make an example of a person who got into an accident and broke their leg, in order for them to get in shape again they need to follow a plan that the doctor will give them in order for them to start learning how to walk again, they start doing small changes every day until they recover. I learned about these small changes when I started my journey of running, seeing someone else do it we think it's easy but it's in the small steps champions take that makes them become better at something, if you consistent then you will notice the changes but it takes time and persistence.

Here are some strategies for self-reflection and growth:

Self-Reflection Strategies:

1. Journaling: Record thoughts, feelings, and experiences.

2. Meditation: Reflect on thoughts, emotions, and behaviours.

3. Self-inquiry: Ask yourself questions (e.g., "What am I grateful for?").

4. Feedback seeking: Ask for constructive feedback from others.

5. Solo retreats: Take time for introspection and self-reflection.

Growth Strategies:

1. Set goals: Establish specific, measurable objectives.

2. Develop a growth mind set: Embrace challenges and learning.

3. Practice self-compassion: Treat yourself with kindness and understanding.

4. Seek new experiences: Engage in novel activities and learning.

5. Build positive habits: Replace negative habits with constructive ones.

Self-Awareness Exercises:

1. Values clarification: Identify core values and priorities.
2. Strengths and weaknesses assessment: Recognize areas for improvement.
3. Emotional intelligence evaluation: Understand emotional patterns.
4. Personality assessments
5. Gratitude practice: Reflect on daily blessings.

Maintaining a positive mind-set in today's world is very crucial because it's easy to get caught up in stress, anxiety and negativity. However maintaining a positive mind set and prioritizing daily wellbeing is crucial for our overall health, happiness & success. While I was on the process of working on myself, cutting down the negativity, it wasn't easy. The thoughts were still there and sometimes I doubted why I was doing the work in the first place because It felt as if I wasn't making progress, but I had to remember why I was on this journey and visualize myself to where I want to be, which allowed me to learn how to maintain a positive mind set, a positive mind set is the foundation of a fulfilling life. When we focus on the good, we attract positivity. A positive attitude goes a long way, Not only does it improve mental health, it reduces stress and enhances relationships.

So we need to practise daily wellbeing but engaging in activities that nourish our mind, body and spirits such as meditation, exercise and time with yourself deepens a connection you have with yourself, take yourself for a date, buy yourself gifts as a reward for your hard work. Neglecting daily wellbeing can lead to a decreased productivity, and poor physical and mental health.

Here are some tips for maintaining a positive mind set and daily well-being:

Morning Routine:

1. Gratitude journaling: Write down 3 things you're thankful for.
2. Positive affirmations: Repeat empowering statements.
3. Morning meditation: 5-10 minutes of mindfulness.
4. Exercise: Stretch or yoga to boost energy.
5. Hydrate: Drink water or herbal tea.

Daily Habits:

1. Practice mindfulness: Focus on the present.
2. Connect with nature: Spend time outdoors.
3. Smile and laugh: Watch a funny video or meme.
4. Healthy eating: Nourish your body with whole foods.
5. Prioritize sleep: 7-8 hours for optimal rest.

Positive Thinking:

1. Reframe negative thoughts: Challenge pessimistic thoughts.
2. Focus on solutions: Approach problems with optimism.
3. Practice self-compassion: Treat yourself with kindness.
4. Celebrate successes: Acknowledge achievements.
5. Visualize positivity: Imagine a bright future.

Self-Care:

1. Schedule downtime: Relax and recharge.
2. Engage in hobbies: Pursue activities that bring joy.
3. Social connections: Nurture relationships.
4. Self-forgiveness: Let go of guilt and shame.
5. Pamper yourself: Enjoy relaxing baths or massages.

Resilience:

1. Practice mindfulness under stress.
2. Develop problem-solving skills.
3. Build a support network.
4. Learn from failures.
5. Focus on the present.

Evening Routine:

1. Reflect on gratitude.
2. Plan for tomorrow.
3. Practice relaxation techniques (deep breathing, progressive muscle relaxation).
4. Disconnect from screens.
5. Prepare for restful sleep.

And finally, Miles Davis said "It's not about standing still and becoming safe. If anybody wants to keep creating they have to be about change."

LOVE,
ME

CLOSINGNOTE

T

'You are the artist of your own life, don't hand the paintbrush to anyone else'

hank you for reaching this far in the book. If you read until here, you've got this, remember that you are unique, capable, and strong. Trust yourself, trust the process, and trust that every step forward is a step closer to your dreams. Congratulations on taking the first step towards maintaining a positive mind set and cutting out the noise, remember this journey is ongoing, and it's essential to be patient, kind and compassionate with yourself. As you close this book, remember that your journey to a more positive and fulfilling life has just begun. The tools, strategies, and insights shared within these pages are meant to guide and support you, not define your path. Thank you for joining me on this journey. Remember, your growth and well-being are worth celebrating.

Final Affirmations:

1. I am enough.
2. I trust myself.
3. I am worthy of love, care, and happiness.
4. I choose positivity and resilience.
5. I celebrate my growth and progress.

Final Reflection:

Take a moment to reflect on your journey so far. Celebrate your successes, acknowledge your challenges, and honour your courage.

"You are the architect of your own happiness; design your life with purpose, passion, and positivity."

Acknowledgments:

Writing a book is harder than I thought but it made me comfortable with the understanding of hard work brings great rewards. None of this would have been possible without my best friend, Oyi. He has been with me since early years of school. He supported me in everything, even when I failed, we failed together and had each other's backs. I'll be forever grateful to have him in my life.

Many special thanks to my friend Kameho Letsae, who was there through times of doubt, times of suffering and pain. She taught me tough love & continues to remind me that I am enough and loved. I truly have no idea where I'd be if she hadn't supported me at times I felt like giving up, I love you always.

To Mr Maphumo, who always saw the best in me throughout my primary school years, he always gave me a voice and made sure I was heard, He never saw my race or age. He saw a kid who wanted to learn, to succeed and have more. He always listened when I had something to say.

A special thanks to Michaela who always supported me in everything including getting in my school work on time. You the best study buddy I could ever ask for

Writing a book about your life' challenges is a process. I'm forever beholden to Olayide Bukola for your editorial help.

Writing this book with you has been a journey that I'll never forget. Much love to Jayson Walker and Donnie for always believing in me, and showing me the way even though I am years younger than you guys, but you treated me like I'm an adult & always supported me through everything that I want to pursue. It is because of their efforts and encouragement that I am where I am today

To everyone at Parivus Studios who enable me to be the Managing Director of a business that I started with no clear vision of where it is now, I am honoured to be a part of the team, and thank you for bringing this company idea I had to life, and for showing up every day and making this a safe space for everyone, but ultimately giving your all into this company.

To my family. To my Dad, for always being supportive and caring throughout all these years I thank you but who I really want to thank is God for blessing me with this man, for your humour and support, even after long hours of work you always come home, whether we In difficult times, Daddy always comes home, you able to work while being present in your family life, you teach me what it means to be a man and I'll carry the lessons forever. To my brother and sister, thank you for always being there when I needed a shoulder to cry on, thank you for the joy shared in laughter and acceptance with one another. To my mom, thank you for always being the person I could confide in during hard times, She strengthened me in ways that I never knew I needed, thank you for the warm food you've always shared with us, thank you for the love you've given me, and always praying for me every day. I love you more than you know.

Finally to all those who have been a part of the journey: To my grandparents, to Samantha W, Anny Liwani, Khazimla Skiti, Lesedi Lebaea, Fiona Montanez, Noni Plaatjie, Shakira Spiers, Tamia Kock, Brian, Kgantsho Naledi, Mire Botha, Abby Tatyana Martin, Lange, Lelethu Gaduka, Mervine, Shekinah, Dimpho Matlala, Thank you for everything without you all I wouldn't be the man that I am today.

Don't miss out!

Visit the website below and you can sign up to receive emails whenever Gideon Faku publishes a new book. There's no charge and no obligation.

https://books2read.com/r/B-A-TSCVC-JDKIF

BOOKS 2 READ

Connecting independent readers to independent writers.

About the Author

Gideon Faku is a passionate advocate for self-expression and empowerment. As a writer, he helps individuals silence their inner critics and unleash their unique voice. With a background in psychology and personal development Gideon draws from his own experiences to inspire others to break free from societal expectations and live unaologetically.

Read more at instagram.com/parivus_films01/.

www.ingramcontent.com/pod-product-compliance
Lightning Source LLC
La Vergne TN
LVHW050554160826
845677LV00011B/2310